D1571407

OFF THE MAP

Wesleyan Poetry in Translation

OFF THE MAP

Selected Poems by Gloria Fuertes

Edited and Translated by
Philip Levine and Ada Long

Wesleyan University Press
Middletown, Connecticut

The translators are grateful to the editors of the following
journals, who published some of these translations: *Poetry East, The
American Poetry Review, The Missouri Review, Antaeus,* and *The
Kenyon Review.*

All inquiries and permissions requests should be addressed to
the Publisher, Wesleyan University Press, 110 Mt. Vernon Street,
Middletown, Connecticut 06457.

Distributed by Harper & Row Publishers, Keystone Industrial Park,
Scranton, Pennsylvania 18512.

Cover photo and photo preceding page 10: Gloria Fuertes in her
study in Madrid.

Library of Congress Cataloging in Publication Data
Fuertes, Gloria. Off the map.
(Wesleyan Poetry in Translation)
I. Fuertes, Gloria—Translations, English.
I. Levine, Philip, 1928–   . II. Long,
Ada. III. Title.
PQ6611.U44A25 1984   861'.62   83-23270
ISBN 0-8195-5102-3 (alk. paper)
ISBN 0-8195-6112-6 (pbk.: alk. paper)

Manufactured in the United States of America
First Edition
First Wesleyan Paperback Edition

Contents

OFF THE MAP

Introduction

Our questions about Gloria Fuertes are likely to be answered some-where in her poems. Each of her books has included at least one and sometimes several poems that are autobiographical, and among these are accounts of her life that read almost like résumés in verse. The facts of a life are part of the basic material of her poetry—poetry rooted in the everyday realities of a particular woman living in a particular time and place. And so she tells us that she was born in 1918 in Madrid. (Actually, she tells us in one poem that she was born in 1920, but later admits she was fibbing.) Her mother was a seamstress from Burgos, her father a worker from Madrid. She was not born into privilege; instead, she was born into poetry. She tells us that she composed poetry before she could read and recited it to the neighborhood kids, as she would later compose poems in the backs of buses or behind the backs of bosses and give readings in the bars of Madrid. She has worked in offices and libraries ("God made me a poet," she says, "and I made myself a librarian"); she has edited children's books and a poetry review; and she has always written poetry.

Although her first book, *Isla Ignorada*, was published in 1950 and she published some seven books during the fifties in either Spain or Latin America, her poetry did not find a large audience in Spain until 1962, with the publication of *Que estás en la tierra*. She has published several books since then, including two volumes of selected works, *Antología poética* (1970) and *Obras incompletas* (1981).

In her poems, Fuertes reminds us frequently of her origins, of her individual identity as a working-class woman. The more of her poetry we read, the more we feel her fierce fidelity to her own identity, which includes the people, the city, and the particular time and world in which she has lived. Her poems do not look back at history, nor do they speak to the future; they look at and speak to people living in this world, now. They speak straight out, in plain language, of the loneliness, restlessness, hard work, dreams and endurance of her own life and the lives around her. She is one woman, alone, but, as she says in her poem "Now," "though tiny, I know many things, / and my body is an endless eye / through which, unfortunately, I see everything." Her poems are detailed accounts of what she sees: an apartment haunted by ghosts and a world haunted by injustice, a crowded mind and crowded streets, the realities of one solitary life linked to the realities of all other solitary lives. Her allegiance is not to a literary movement or to other poets or to posterity but to herself and the world she sees around her—a world that desperately needs to see itself through poetry. And so, she says, the poet must write frankly and clearly, so that everyone can understand.

The world Fuertes sees contains much that is wrong, and what she writes about it is both frank and clear. Hers are not poems of doubt, uncertainty, qualification or ambiguity. What is right is right, what is wrong is wrong, and all you have to do to see the difference is look. A lover to wake up next to, a pencil that will write, a sturdy pair of shoes, the beauty of a new butterfly, the stubbornness of a goat, a glass of wine, a full stomach and a full heart—these things are right. Their absence is wrong. This is a world in which too much is absent too often, and most absent of all is natural feeling, openly expressed. The prevailing sin of and against humanity is indifference. The rich ignore the poor; the employer ignores the worker; men and women ignore each other; even God sometimes hides in his heaven like a businessman hiding in the suburbs of Madrid. Underlying this general indifference is the power of possession, the displacement of love from people to things, and so the feeling creatures on earth are the dispossessed—beggars, abandoned lovers, animals, corpses, ghosts and poets—and for them it's hard going.

In one of her poems ("Prayer: Come In"), Fuertes asks God to allow her to share in the general indifference so that she can be like everyone else. But clearly this is one of those prayers that God didn't hear, for one of the constant elements in Fuertes's poetry is the pain—and every once in a while the joy—of being different in an indifferent world. In her love poetry, the difference is cause for exuberance; she goes wild on love, describing it with unqualified and unashamed hyperbole. In "When I Hear Your Name," for instance, we see a woman joyously love-crazed, freed from the monotony of moderation, refusing constraint in an extravagant totality of feeling. But much more often in her poetry, we see a woman who has no one with whom to share her feeling, a woman wholly alone, often enclosed within her apartment, without possessions, without friends, without a man.

The prevalent feeling in Fuertes's poems is loneliness. But, in the best of her poetry, she never wastes her loneliness on self-pity. In the absence of human love, the impulse to share does not diminish, and so the emptiness fills with a remarkable variety of companions. Sometimes the companions are quiet, as in "Today Is Sunday," a poem as spare as the life it describes.

> Today is Sunday.
> The quiet little afternoon lies beside me.
>
> As always, I am at home,
> with three things that have no bodies,
> a memory,
> a letter,
> a photo of my mother.

But more often the companions are noisy, filling the silence with the sounds of uninvented instruments or "the cries of the just born" ("Lonely Room"). Ghosts come around in garments that need mending and howl in the attic or crack walnuts in her head ("Society of Friends and Protectors"). These restless and needy ghosts are perfectly natural and familiar to her; what is unnatural, and what she cannot get used to, is the indifference of men.

Time and again in her poems, Fuertes portrays the natural affection of animals and even objects to indict man's indifference. The pathetic fallacy is no fallacy in her poetry but a correction of the fallacious logic that would attribute feelings only to human beings when, of all God's creations, they have the least. The impulse to share and to give is universal throughout the natural world; the absence of that impulse in men is the one disruptive element in the world and in her life and poems. "Birds Nest," for instance, devotes nine lines to the affection of creatures who come to her and make her part of their world, make her useful and real, but the tenth and final line twists the poem out of joint with its introduction of "men" who "think I'm nothing." Similarly, in "Wild Ballad" Fuertes tells of the love between the gazelle and the stag, the rock and the moss, the sea and the land, and concludes:

> All of these love freely.
> Only man blooms for himself.
> The gazelle and the stag stop
> in the deepening shadows of the lime trees.

Man has only a one-line appearance, but he steals the show.

On the streets of Madrid, among the poor and lonely, Fuertes sometimes finds a world in tune with nature. In "Prayer: Our Father" and "Instructions," the lives of the workers are blessed by the presence of God, or by angels who "raise the moon / as though it were a political banner." But most often her city poems are angry poems — angry because God, like a rich man, chooses to absent himself from the lives of the poor, the aged, the sick, the exhausted. She looks around her and sees a world where people get what they don't need. The people with clothes get more clothes; the overworked get more work. A man works sixteen hours a day for a lifetime in order to make less than "those jocks make in an afternoon / kicking a ball around" ("A Man's Going"). Korean children are served up in white sauce to officials who issue posters prohibiting the consumption of fried birds ("It's Useless"). The world is upside down, and the people who are down have got to start setting the world right by screaming, disobeying, and refusing to stay down.

In defying tyranny, Fuertes's poems attack its major cause, which is separation — the separation between man and nature, between rich and poor, between God and man. The best solution lies in proximity, familiarity, and equality, and all three are prominent in the tone and content of her work. She is on equally familiar terms with beggars, rich men, insects, ghosts, death, God, and her living-room chair. Nothing or no one gets special privileges; the standards of right and wrong apply equally to all. So when God is here on earth where he belongs, she speaks to him with love and respect; when he hides out in his heaven, she tells him to come down here and get to work. In both cases she addresses him as an accessible presence in her daily life. She sees her relationship to him as one of mutual responsibility, so when she doesn't see him holding up his end, she calls him "the Great What's His Name" ("The Skinny Women").

The fearlessness of her response to God extends to all the world's mysteries, both natural and supernatural. Death, corpses, and ghosts are everyday companions — amiable, gossipy, and domestic. What the world finds remote and mysterious, she accepts as normal. But what the world accepts as normal, she finds infinitely mysterious. There's nothing special about the three Magi from the East — they're typical businessmen anxious to get to an appointment on time — but the obstinate endurance of their camel is truly marvelous. Marvelous also is the pleasure of a new hairdo, for this is a sign of blessedness. The ultimate consolation she has for a dead man in his bed is that his "hair is perfect," and she ends her poem "Here I Am Exposed Like Everybody" with the lines:

> What I have in common with a saint
> or beggar is loving one person above all things,
> never having any shoes, and knowing
> someday God will come down to do my hair.

The greatest miracles are performed daily on earth, and she feels sorry for God because he cannot throw rocks at streetlights or skip school or put on a new hat to go to mass ("What Would Become of God without Us?").

As Fuertes finds the greatest wonder in the simplest things, so does she perceive the most complex mysteries in the simplest sentences. There is something mystifying, even frightening, about the capacity of basic syntactic structures to impose logic where there is none and to express incomprehensible truths in the form of factual statements. In "Grammatical Sentences" she draws our attention specifically to this paradox in a series of simple statements: "I have hope. / The dog has hunger" and "The flowers in the suburbs are evil / The flowerpots are boats" and "Orphans smell of their mothers, / the poor of smoke, / the rich of tar." Simple grammatical substitutions can release all the mysterious possibilities for good and evil, love and injustice, beauty and violence in the common materials and language of our lives. And so the simple statement is the basis of Fuertes's style: plain sentences in plain language, the language all people use.

The forms of her poems are also simple, and range from the traditional lyric to forms that seem antithetical to poetry. I have already mentioned her biographical sketches, which often play on the form of a job application. Others of her poems take the form of business letters or appeals for redress of grievances. Many of her poems are prayers and adopt standard liturgical formats. Her poems often have a specific listener, such as God or a rich man or a corpse; if she dislikes the listener, she frequently adopts an ironically formal approach, but if she likes him, she usually chats. The cadence of real conversations between real people is an essential part of her poetics.

But even the simplest of forms becomes, in Fuertes's poetry, a vehicle for personal and political statements that are hardly simple; they are clear but not easy. A form that recurs again and again in her poems, for instance, is the list: her list of grammatical sentences, the street hawker's catalogue of his merchandise, the newspaper's itemized account of the contents of an ostrich's stomach, a list of side shows at a fair. Seemingly random accounts of "things" reveal more than her taste for the haphazard and the heterogeneous. They also reveal a love of names, of the magical power of naming—the same love that Homer, Milton, and Joyce revealed in their lengthy catalogues of boats, trees, and public figures. Not just the names, but the things themselves become a source of wonder, revealing her living relationship with simple objects. But the relationship has its melancholy side. The very randomness of the lists—in which merry-go-rounds, tricycles, singing seals and poets are all thrown in together—bespeaks an absence of order that is at the same time exhilarating and overwhelming. And, in that absence of order, the lists reveal the loneliness and restlessness of the observer, who has a place that is everyplace and noplace, who wanders the length of the carnival and—unfortunately—sees everything.

Being poet, woman, and working-class is triple jeopardy in this world, but in the poems of Gloria Fuertes it is a powerful combination. Out of solitude, anonymity, and displacement, there emerges a voice in her poems that is familiar, personal, passionate, compassionate, and uncompromisingly egalitarian. Above all, the voice is strong. Fuertes is certain she will be heard, that poetry is powerful, that she is powerful. Defying every form of exploitation, cynicism, and indifference, she insists on faith—faith in the possibility of a free world of feeling individuals who acknowledge the bonds of sympathy and responsibility to one another. In her poems, she does her part to bring that world into being.

Ada Long

Gloria Fuertes in her study in Madrid.

Autobiografía

A los pies de la Catedral de Burgos,
nació mi madre.
A los pies de la Catedral de Madrid,
nació mi padre.
Yo nací a los pies de mi madre
en el centro de España, una tarde.
Mi padre era obrero,
modista mi madre.
Yo quisiera haber sido del circo
y sólo soy esto.
De pequeña,
fui a un reformatorio y a un colegio gratis
De joven fui al dolor
y en el verano a un Preventorio,
ahora voy a todas partes.
He tenido lo menos siete amores,
varios jefes malos
y apetito envidiable.
Ahora tengo, dos recordatorios
y un beso de tarde en tarde.

Autobiography

At the foot of the Cathedral of Burgos
my mother was born.
At the foot of the Cathedral of Madrid
my father was born.
At the foot of my mother I was born
one afternoon in the middle of Spain.
My father was a worker,
my mother was a seamstress.
I wanted to take off with the circus
but I'm only what I am.
When I was little
I went to a reformatory and a free school.
As a kid I was sickly
and summered in a sanatorium,
but now I get around.
I've had at least seven love affairs,
some bad daddies,
and a marvelous appetite.
Now I've got two minor convictions
and a kiss from time to time.

Ahora

Ahora, voy a contaros
cómo fue que los gusanos
que mantenía con hojas de morera
en una caja vacía de jabón,
se me convirtieron
en bolas alargadas de colores,
y cómo después yo los vi
transfigurarse en mariposas,
y esto sucedió porque era mayo sólo
y los insectos son así de mágicos.

Luego os contaré
de cómo Eloisa Muro,
cuarta querida de Cervantes,
fue la que escribió el Quijote.

Porque yo, tan mínima, sé tantas cosas,
y mi cuerpo es un ojo sin fin
con el que para mi desventura veo todo.

Now

Now I'm going to tell you
how the worms
I fed on mulberry leaves
in an empty soap carton
changed themselves without my help
into long fluffs of color,
and how later I saw them
transformed into butterflies,
and all this because it was May
and insects are, in their way, magicians.

I'll tell you
how Eloisa Muro,
the fourth mistress of Cervantes,
wrote *Don Quixote*.

Because though tiny, I know many things,
and my body is an endless eye
through which, unfortunately, I see everything.

Es Inútil

Inútil que a estas fechas
nos empiece a dar pena de la rosa y el pájaro,
inútil que encendamos velas por los pasillos,
inútil que nos prohiban nada,
no hablar por ejemplo,
comer carne,
beber libros,
bajarnos sin pagar en el tranvía,
querer a varios seres,
fumar yerbas,
decir verdades,
amar al enemigo,
inútil es que nos prohiban nada.

En los diarios vienen circulares,
papeles hay pegados en la esquina
que prohiben comer pájaros fritos;
¡y no prohiben comer hombres asados,
con dientes de metralla comer hombres desnudos!

¿Por qué prohiben pájaros los mismos que consienten
ejecutar al séptimo y al quinto mandamiento?
Tampoco han prohibido los niños en Corea
y se los sigue el hombre comiendo en salsa blanca.

La Protectora de Animales está haciendo el ridículo.

Tampoco han prohibido comer las inocentes pescadillas,
los tiernos y purísimos corderos,
las melancólicas lubinas,
las perdices,

It's Useless

It's useless at this date
to start punishing the rose and the bird,
useless to burn candles in the hallways,
useless to prohibit anything,
like speaking,
eating meat,
drinking books,
traveling for nothing on the streetcars,
desiring certain creatures,
smoking grass,
telling the truth,
loving your enemy,
it's a waste of time to prohibit anything.

There are announcements in the papers,
there are posters stuck on every corner
that prohibit the eating of fried birds,
but they never stop the roasting of men,
the eating of naked men with a gun's hunger.

Why are birds protected by those
who execute the seventh and fifth commandments?
Have they protected the Korean children?
Men go on eating them in white sauce.

The Patron of Animals is making a fool of herself.

Have they stopped the eating of innocent fish,
the pure and tender lambs,
the sad sea bass,
partridges?

y qué me dices
de Mariquita Pérez
que la compran abrigos de trescientas pesetas
habiendo tanta niña sin muñeca ni ropa.
Los enfermos trabajan,
los ancianos ejercen,
el opio en tal café puede comprarse,
la joventud se vende,
todo esto está oficialmente permitido.
Comprended y pensad, nada se arregla con tener buenos sentimientos;
hay que tener arranque y ganas de gritar:
— ¡Mientras haya guerras comeré pájaros fritos!

And what can you say
about Mariquita Pérez
for whom expensive coats are bought
while there are girls without dolls or clothes?
The sick work,
the old exercise,
they sell heroin in all the bars,
teen-agers are for sale,
and all this goes on officially.
Get it straight, nobody does anything just because he's good-hearted.
You've got to go nuts and start screaming:
"As long as you murder, I'll eat fried birds!"

He Dormido

He dormido en el andén del metro,
—por miedo al despellejo de metralla—,
he dormido en el borde de la playa
y en el borde del borde del tintero.

He dormido descalza y sin sombrero
sin muñeca ni sábana de arriba
me he dormido sentada en una silla
—y amanecí en el suelo—.

Y la noche después de los desahucios
y los días después del aguacero,
dormía entre estropajas y asperones
en la tienda del tío cacharrero.

Crecí, me puse larga regordeta,
me desvelé, pero seguí durmiendo,
llegué a mocita dicen que a poeta,
y terminé durmiéndome al sereno.

Y a pesar de estos golpes de fortuna
ya veréis por qué tengo buen talento;

he dormido a las penas una a una,
y he dormido en el pecho de mi amante.

I've Slept

I've slept on the subway platform,
—afraid of the torn skins of shrapnel—
I've slept on the edge of the sea
and on the tip of the tongue of the inkwell.

I've slept barefooted and bareheaded
without a doll, without a sheet to cover me,
I've slept in a chair, upright,
and wakened later on the ground.

And the night we were put out on the streets
and the days after the storms broke,
I slept between scrub brushes and grindstones
in the old man's secondhand store.

I grew up till I was tall and swelled my clothes,
I kept my eye out, and still I went on sleeping,
became a young lady, became—they say—a poet,
and wound up sleeping out in the night.

And in spite of all the luck of hard knocks
you can see why I'm so talented;

one by one I've sent my troubles off to bed,
and slept myself beside my lover man.

Cuando Te Nombran

Cuando te nombran,
me roban un poquito de tu nombre;
parece mentira,
que media docena de letras digan tanto.

Mi locura sería deshacer las murallas con tu nombre,
iría pintando todas las paredes,
no quedaría un pozo
sin que yo me asomara
para decir tu nombre,
ni montaña de piedra
donde yo no gritara
enseñándole al eco
tus seis letras distintas.

Mi locura sería,
enseñar a las aves a cantarlo,
enseñar a los peces a beberlo,
enseñar a los hombres que no hay nada,
como volverse loco y repetir tu nombre.

Mi locura sería olvidarme de todo,
de las 22 letras restantes, de los números,
de los libros leídos, de los versos creados.
Saludar con tu nombre.
Pedir pan con tu nombre.
—Siempre dice lo mismo—dirían a mi paso,
y yo, tan orgullosa, tan feliz, tan campante.

Y me iré al otro mundo con tu nombre en la boca,
a todas las preguntas responderé tu nombre
—los jueces y los santos no van a entender nada—.
Dios me condenaría a decirlo sin parar para siempre.

When I Hear Your Name

When I hear your name
I feel a little robbed of it;
it seems unbelievable
that half a dozen letters could say so much.

My compulsion is to blast down every wall with your name,
I'd paint it on all the houses,
there wouldn't be a well
I hadn't leaned into
to shout your name there,
nor a stone mountain
where I hadn't uttered
those six separate letters
that are echoed back.

My compulsion is
to teach the birds to sing it,
to teach the fish to drink it,
to teach men that there is nothing
like the madness of repeating your name.

My compulsion is to forget altogether
the other 22 letters, all the numbers,
the books I've read, the poems I've written.
To say hello with your name.
To beg bread with your name.
"She always says the same thing," they'd say when they saw me,
and I'd be so proud, so happy, so self-contained.

And I'll go to the other world with your name on my tongue,
and all their questions I'll answer with your name
—the judges and saints will understand nothing—
God will sentence me to repeating it endlessly and forever.

El Amor Te Convierte en Rosal

El amor te convierte en rosal
y en el pecho te nace
esa espina robusta como un clavo
donde el demonio cuelga su uniforme.

Al tocar lo que amas te quemas en los dedos,
y sigues sigues sigues hasta abrasarte todo;
después,
      ya en pie de nuevo,
tu cuerpo es otra cosa,
  . . . es la estatua de un héroe muerto en algo,
al que no se le ven las cicatrices.

Love Turns You into a Rosebush

Love turns you into a rosebush
and your heart grows
a thorn as big as a spike
from which the devil hangs his costume.

Playing with the parts you love you scorch your fingers,
and you go on and on and on until you're all ashes;
later,
      on your feet again,
your body's something else.
. . . the statue of a hero who dies somehow or other,
and none of the wounds show.

Cuarto de Soltera

Por mi casa sin amo
suena un instrumento que aún no se ha inventado.
Y alguna vez consigo ver a un diablo
con una regadera llena de vino blanco.
De noche, alguien se queja por mi lado.
¡Aves del otro mundo
se vienen a morir a mi tejado!
De madrugada, el silencio es demasiado.
Luego vuelve a sonar el instrumento desafinado.
¡Mi cuarto de soltera está embrujado!
De todas sus esquinas salen llantos
de niños recién manipulados.
Todo esto sucede y otras cosas
en mi casa sin amo.

Lonely Room

In my house without a man
an instrument sings that's not been invented.
Sometimes I see a devil
with a watering can of white wine,
at night someone grumbles by my side.
The birds of another world
come to die on my roof!
Before dawn, the silence is too much.
Out of tune, it begins again.
My maidenly room is bewitched!
From every corner come
the cries of the just born.
All of this and more
In my house without a man.

Sociedad de Amigos y Protectores

Sociedad de Amigos y Protectores
de Espectros, Fantasmas y Trasgos.

Muy señores suyos:
Tengo el disgusto de comunicarles
que tengo en casa y a su disposición
un fantasma pequeño
de unos dos muertos de edad,
que habla polaco y dice ser el espíritu del Gengis Kan.
Viste sábana blanca de pesca
con matrícula de Uranio
y lleva un siete en el dobladillo
que me da miedo zurcírselo
porque no se está quieto.

Aparece al atardecer,
o de mañana si el día está nublado
y por las noches cabalga por mis hombros
o se mete en mi cabeza a machacar nueces.
Con mi perro se lleva a matar
y a mí me está destrozando los nervios.
Dice que no se va porque no le da la gana.

Todos los días hace que se me vaya la leche,
me esconde el cepillo, la paz y las tijeras;
si alguna vez tengo la suerte
de conciliar el sueño,
ulula desgañitándose por el desván.

Ruego a ustedes manden lo que tengan que mandar,
y se lleven de mi honesto pisito
a dicho ente,
antes de que le coja cariño.

Society of Friends and Protectors

To the Society of Friends and Protectors
of Spirits, Ghosts, and Goblins.

Dear Sirs:
I have the sad duty to inform you
that in my apartment and at your disposal
I have a little ghost
some two deads old
who speaks Polish and claims to be the ghost of Genghis Khan.
He's dressed in a plain fishing net
stamped "Made in Uranus"
and torn in the hem,
which I'm afraid to mend
because he won't hold still.

He appears in the late afternoon
or in the morning on cloudy days,
and at night he rides me piggyback
or crawls inside my head and cracks walnuts.
He starts fights with the dog,
and he's making me a nervous wreck.
He won't leave, he says, because he doesn't feel like it.

Every day he disappears with my milk,
he hides my hairbrush, my peace of mind, my scissors;
when I'm lucky enough
to fall asleep
he howls through the attic with all his might.

I beg of you to do what must be done
to get out of my apartment
this thing I've spoken of
before I start to fall for him.

Aquí Estoy Expuesta Como Todos

Aquí estoy expuesta como todos,
con una mano ya en el otro mundo,
con una suave cuerdo en la garganta
que me da música y me quita sangre.
Esto de escribir esto es horroroso,
—un día moriré de amar a alguien—,
lo llaman ser poeta y es ser santo,
nadie nos canoniza pero andamos,
con raras aureolas por las sienes,
por las noches a veces relucimos,
con invisibles seres conversamos,
apariciones múltiples tenemos
y dormimos sentados en la sala.
Nos desprecian los jefes, se nos ríen
detrás los empleados,
y los perros nos siguen por las calles.
Que yo tengo de santo y de mendigo
esto de amar a un ser sobre las cosas
esto de no tener nunca zapatos
y esto de que Dios baje por peinarme.

Here I Am Exposed Like Everybody

Here I am exposed like everybody,
with one hand already in the other world,
with a subtle cord at my throat
that makes music and draws my blood.
This writing thing is awful —
someday I'll die of loving someone —
they call it being a poet but it's being a saint.
We're not canonized, but we go around
with strange halos over our heads,
at night we sometimes glow brilliantly,
we have conversations with unseen creatures,
we see apparitions all the time,
and we sleep sitting up in the living room.
Our bosses despise us, our fellow workers
laugh at us behind our backs,
and only dogs follow us on the streets.
What I have in common with a saint
or beggar is loving one person above all things,
never having any shoes, and knowing
someday God will come down to do my hair.

Balada Salvaje

A Lucinda, que tanto ama a los versos

Qué amor más sano había
entre el ciervo y aquella gacelilla.

Se encontraban al alba junto al lago,
se corrían saltando todo el día.

Su amor fue como el agua del arroyo,
¡qué cristalino amor ay, les unía!
La gacela y el ciervo paseaban
por el bosque besándose en la umbría.

Desinteresado amor les unía.
En el mundo animal
pasan las cosas
más bellas de la vida.

Un pájaro que canta a la paloma;
un lagarto que espera noche y día...
—una gacela hermosa se estremece,
porque el ciervo la mira—.

La roca tiene amores con el musgo,
la pared con la hiedra.
El árbol se conmueve con la brisa
el mar ama a la tierra.

Y todo tiene amores para nada.
Sólo del hombre brota el egoísmo.
La gacela y el ciervo se han parado,
bajo la sombra espesa de los tilos....

Wild Ballad

For Lucinda, who so loves poetry

Between the stag and the little gazelle
there is no more perfect love.

At dawn they meet beside the lake
and skip a whole day frisking together.

Their love is like the water of the arroyo.
How clear that which brought them together!
The gazelle and the stag walk through
the forest kissing each other in the shadows.

Unselfish love joined them.
The nicest things
in life take place
in the animal world.

A bird sings to a dove,
a lizard waits all night and day . . .
a beautiful gazelle trembles
because the stag beholds her.

The rock loves the moss,
the wall loves the ivy,
the tree shivers in the wind,
the sea strokes the land.

All of these love freely.
Only man blooms for himself.
The gazelle and the stag stop
in the deepening shadows of the lime trees. . . .

Enseñanzas

Aprendamos por fin de las tinieblas,
de las bestias,
imitemos las formas de las flores,
de los insectos aprendamos vida
y de la hierba danza.
Conozcamos la paz de los salvajes.
Anochece la tarde;
el mendigo "echa el cierre" recoge su pañuelo,
una veinte a la hora a veces saca.
La Luisa anda enredada con el Pepe.
Tere la castañera escupe raro
y su hijo el botones se hace golfo,
y por lo demás aquí no pasa nada.
Anochece decía.
Dos ángeles al fin izan la luna
cual si fuera bandera de un partido.

Instructions

Let us learn at last from the darkness,
from the animals,
let us imitate the manners of the flowers,
from the insects let us learn life,
and from the grass, dance.
Let us understand the peace of savages.
The afternoon darkens;
the beggar closes up shop, gathers his handkerchief,
on which he sometimes clears two bits an hour.
Our Luisa passes wrapped around her Pepe.
Tere, the chestnut seller, spits from her bad lungs,
and her son, the bellhop, pretends he's tough.
As I was saying last night,
That's all that goes on here.
At last two angels raise the moon
as though it were a political banner.

Las Flacas Mujeres

Las flacas mujeres de los metalúrgicos
siguen pariendo en casa o en el tranvía.
Los niños van algunos a las Escuelas Municipales
y se aprenden los ríos porque es cosa que gusta.
Las niñas van a las monjas que enseñan sus labores y a rezar.
De la ciudad se va borrando poco a poco la huella
    de los morteros.
¡Han pasado tantos meses!
. . . .

He visto en sueños que hay varios señores
hablando en una mesa de divisas,
de barcos, de aviones, de cornisas
que se van a caer cuando las bombas.

Y yo pido perdón al Gran Quien Sea
por desearles una buena caja,
con cuatro cirios de los más curiosos.

The Skinny Women

The skinny women of the foundry workers
keep on hatching at home or on the streetcar.
Some of the boys go to the public schools
and learn the rivers by heart because it's nice to know.
The girls go to the nuns who teach them girl work and praying.
Bit by bit the traces of mortar fire are wiped from the city.
And the months go by!

. . . .

In dreams I've seen several Mister Bigs
talking around a table about exchange rates,
about ships, planes, about the cornices
that are going to collapse when the bombs drop.

And I beg pardon of the Great What's His Name
for wishing them each a good pine box
and four of the most expensive candles.

Labrador

Labrador,
ya eres más de la tierra que del pueblo.
Cuando pasas, tu espalda huele a campo.
Ya barruntas la lluvia y te esponjas,
ya eres casi de barro.
De tanto arar, ya tienes dos raíces
debajo de tus pies heridos y anchos.

Madrugas, labrador, y dejas tierra
de huella sobre el sitio de tu cama,
a tu mujer le duele la cintura
por la tierra que dejas derramada.
Labrador, tienes tierra en los oídos,
entre las uñas tierra, en las entrañas;
labrador, tienes chepa bajo el hombro
y es tierra acumulada,
te vas hacia la tierra siendo tierra,
los terrones te tiran de la barba.

Ya no quiere que siembres más semillas,
que quiere que te siembres y te vayas,
que el hijo te releve en la tarea;
ya estás mimetizado con la parva,
estás hecho ya polvo con el polvo
de la trilla y la tralla.

Te has ganado la tierra con la tierra;
no quiere verte viejo en la labranza,
te abre los brazos bella por el surco,
échate en ella, labrador, descansa.

Farmer

Farmer,
you already belong to the ground more than the village.
When you go by, your back smells of the fields.
You feel the rain's coming, and then you soak it up
until you're almost turned to clay.
From so much plowing, you've sunk two roots
down from your splayed feet.

Waking before dawn, you leave dirt
to mark the place you've slept,
the same earth that, spread out,
grinds the belly of your woman.
Farmer, you carry the earth in your ears,
and earth under your fingernails, in your intestines;
you bend under a humped back
that is dirt packed down;
being dirt, you're drawn to dirt,
little clods of dirt dribble from your beard.

The earth doesn't want you to sow anymore.
Scatter the seeds you have and plant yourself,
so that your son can take up the work;
already you look like the ripe grain of the harvest;
you can become dust with the dust
of the winnow and the wind.

You've earned this earth with earth;
it doesn't want to see you broken by work.
In the deep furrows it opens its arms to you;
lie down, old man, lie down and rest.

Soy Sólo una Mujer

Soy sólo una mujer y ya es bastante,
con tener una chiva, una tartana
un "bendito sea Dios" por la mañana
y un mico en el pescante.

Yo quisiera haber sido delineante,
o delirante Safo sensitiva
y heme,
aquí,
que soy una perdida
entre tanto mangante.
Lo digo para todo el que me lea,
quise ser capitán, sin arma alguna,
depositar mis versos en la luna
y un astronauta me pisó la idea.

De PAZ por esos mundos quise ser traficante
—me detuvieron por la carretera—
soy sólo una mujer, de cuerda entera,
soy sólo una mujer y ya es bastante.

I'm Only a Woman

I'm only a woman, and that's enough,
with a goat and an old car,
a "Praise the Lord" every morning,
and a lecherous fool running the show.

I wish I'd been a designer,
or a raving, sensitive Sappho,
look at me
here,
lost
among all these slobs.
I say this for anyone who reads me,
I wanted to be a commander without weapons,
to plant my poems on the moon,
but an astronaut beat me to it.

I wanted to be a pusher of peace on earth—
they arrested me on the road—
I'm only a woman, a full-blooded one,
I'm only a woman, and that's enough.

Hoy Es Domingo

Hoy es domingo.
La tarde quietecita está a mi lado.

Yo, como siempre, en mi casa,
con tres seres sin carne,
un recuerdo,
una carta
y un retrato de mi madre.

Today Is Sunday

Today is Sunday.
The quiet little afternoon lies beside me.

As always, I am at home,
with three things that have no bodies,
a memory,
a letter,
a photo of my mother.

Escalando

La Muerte estaba allí sentada al borde,
—la Muerte que yo vi no era delgada,
ni huesuda, ni fría,
ni en sudario envolvía su espesa cabellera—.

La Muerte estaba sola como siempre,
haciéndose un chaleco de ganchillo,
sentada en una piedra de la roca,
estaba distraída, no debió verme,
en seguida gritó: "¡No te tocaba!"
y se puso a tejer como una loca.

—Podrás llevarte entonces estos versos,
estas ganas de amar y este cigarro
podrás llevarte el cuerpo que me duele
pero cuidado con tocar mi alma.

A la Muerte la tengo pensativa
porque no ha conseguido entristecerme.

Climbing

Death was there, sitting by the roadside
— the Death I saw wasn't skinny,
or all bones, or freezing,
and she didn't shroud her thick hair in a rag.

As usual Death was alone,
sitting on a rock of the crag
knitting herself a sweater.
She was so busy she didn't see me,
right off she shouted, "It's not your turn!"
and started knitting like mad.

—OK, you can take these poems away,
this wanting love and this cigarette,
you can take this body that's killing me,
but be careful not to finger my soul.

I've got Death really thinking
because she couldn't make me sad.

¿Qué Sería de Dios sin Nosotros?

Lo más triste de Dios
es que no puede creer en Dios.
Ni ponerse el sombrero nuevo
para ir a misa como tú y como yo.
Tampoco puede dar gracias al Señor,
ni hacer novillos
ni tirar una piedra a una farol.

¿Qué sería sin nosotros de Dios?

What Would Become of God without Us?

The saddest thing about God
is that he can't believe in God.
He can't put on his new hat
as we can and go to mass.
Neither can he thank the Almighty,
or skip school,
or throw a rock at a streetlight.

What would become of God without us?

Virgen de Plástico

Con su manto de nylon
y la corona eléctrica,
con pilas en el pecho
y una sonrisa triste,
se la ve en las vitrinas de todos los comercios
y en los sucios hogares de los pobres católicos.
En Nueva York los negros
tienen su virgen blanca
presidiendo el lavabo
junto a la cabecera...
Es un cruce de Virgen entre Fátima y Lourdes,
un leve vaciado con troquel "made in USA,"
tiene melena larga y las manos abiertas
es lavable y si cae no se descascarilla.
Las hay de tres colores,
blancas, azules, rosas
—las hay de tres tamaños—
—aún la grande es pequeña—.
Así, sin angelitos,
Virgen de resultado,
me diste tanta pena,
Virgen pura de plástico,
se me quitó le gana
de pedirte un milagro.

Plastic Virgin

With her nylon veil
and electric crown,
with her dry-cell batteries
in her breast, and a dismal smile,
she's on display in all the shops
and on the dusty shelves of poor Catholics.
In New York City, above the bedstead
this white virgin watches over
the washstands of Negroes...
Crossbreed of Fátima and Lourdes,
lightweight model stamped "Made in USA,"
with streaming hair and open hands,
she's washable and shatterproof.
Comes in three colors
—white, pink, and blue—
available in three sizes
though even the big one is small.
There, without angels,
virgin Virgin,
I've felt so bad for you,
pure Virgin of plastic,
I can't bring myself
to ask for one miracle.

¡Hago Versos, Señores!

Hago versos, señores, hago versos,
pero no me gusta que me llamen poetisa,
me gusta el vino como a los albañiles
y tengo una asistenta que habla sola.
Este mundo resulta divertido,
pasan cosas señores que no expongo,
se dan casos, aunque nunca se dan casas
a los pobres que no pueden dar traspaso.

Sigue habiendo solteras con su perro,
sigue habiendo casados con querida
a los déspotas duros nadie les dice nada,
y leemos que hay muertos y pasamos la hoja,
y nos pisan el cuello y nadie se levanta,
y nos odia la gente y decimos: ¡la vida!

Esto pasa señores y yo debo decirlo.

I Write Poems

I write poems, gentlemen, I write poems,
but don't call me poetess;
I like my wine like the bricklayers do,
and I have a helper who talks
to herself. It's a crazy world;
things happen I don't want to talk about,
gentlemen; there are cases . . . however they
never give houses to the poor who don't have them.

There are always old maids walking their dogs
and proper husbands walking their girl friends;
to the petty tyrants no one talks back;
we read the deaths and turn the pages;
they step on our necks and we don't get up;
the people hate us and we say, "That's life!"

All this happens, gentlemen, and I must say it.

La Ida del Hombre

Setenta años es mucho,
muero viejo,
cansado de trabajar,
dieciséis horas últimamente,
y no he ganado en toda mi vida
lo que gana un jugador en una tarde
dando patadas a un balón.
Por este bienestar, y esta armonía,
que me sube del pie a la garganta
sé que muero,
y esta tonta de mujer anda llorando,
nunca tuvo idea de los acontecimientos.
Buena vida para los dos se abre.
Noto empiezo a encogerme;
he de nacer de nuevo parido de esta madre que es la muerte;
ya no te despertará mi tos de madrugada,
ya no pasaré más frío en la obra,
se cicatrizarán mis sabañones,
podrás desempeñar (1) las mantas
con lo que te dé el Montepío,
mujer (2), no es motivo que llores por tan poca cosa.

(1) Variante: podrás empeñar.
(2) Variante: mujer, hazte cargo.

A Man's Going

Seventy years is plenty;
I'm dying an old man
wiped out by work,
sixteen hours a day, even at the end,
and in my whole life I never made
what those jocks make in an afternoon
kicking a ball around.
This sense of well-being, this peace
that climbs from my toes to my throat
tells me I'm a goner,
and my dumb woman goes around crying,
but she's never known the score.
There's a good life opening for the two of us.
I notice I'm starting to shrivel up,
I've got to be born all over, mothered this time by death.
Now my coughing won't wake you at 4:00 A.M.
I won't be freezing on the job,
my chilblains will heal at last;
with what you get from Social Security
you'll be able to get the blankets out of hock.
Woman, wise up, it's no use bawling over nothing.

Oración

Que estás en la tierra, Padre nuestro,
que te siento en la púa del pino,
en el torso azul del obrero,
en la niña que borda curvada
la espalda, mezclando el hilo en el dedo.
Padre nuestro que estás en la tierra,
en el surco,
en el huerto,
en la mina,
en el puerto,
en el cine,
en el vino,
en la casa del médico.
Padre nuestro que estás en la tierra,
donde tienes tu gloria y tu infierno
y tu limbo que está en los cafés
donde los pudientes beben su refresco.
Padre nuestro que estás en la escuela de gratis,
y en el verdulero,
y en el que pasa hambre
y en el poeta, ¡nunca en el usurero!
Padre nuestro que estás en la tierra,
en un banco del Prado leyendo,
eres ese Viejo que da migas de pan a los pájaros del paseo.
Padre nuestro que estás en la tierra,
en el cigarro, en el beso,
en la espiga, en el pecho
de todos los que son buenos.
Padre que habitas en cualquier sitio.
Dios que penetras en cualquier hueco,
tú que quitas la angustia, que estás en la tierra,
Padre nuestro que sí que te vemos
los que luego te hemos de ver,
donde sea, o ahí en el cielo.

Prayer

Our Father who I know is on earth,
whom I feel in the pine needle,
in the blue shirt of the worker,
in the child bent over her embroidery
winding the thread around a finger.
Our Father who is on earth,
in the furrow,
in the orchard,
in the mine,
in the doorway,
in the movies,
in the wine,
in the doctor's office.
Our Father who is on earth,
where you keep your glory and your hell
and your limbo, which is in the cafes
where the rich drink together.
Our Father who is in the public school,
in the fruit seller,
and in those who go hungry,
and in the poet, but never in the banker.
Our Father who is on earth,
on a park bench in the Prado, reading,
you are the old man who tosses bread to the street birds.
Our Father who is on earth,
in the cigar, in the kiss,
in the ear of corn, in the heart
of all those who are decent.
Father who lives anywhere,
God who penetrates all emptiness,
you who end pain, who is on earth,
our Father whom now we see,
we who will soon see you again
here or in heaven.

No Tengo Nunca Nada

No tengo nada nunca en mi gris monedero,
tampoco nunca nada que ponerme elegante,
siempre llevo los mismos zapatos sin cordones,
y a veces fumo negro y nada importa nada.

Tengo un cristal clavado debajo de la lengua
y un nuevo ser... Observad que voy a hablaros de un nuevo ser.

¿Qué caduco ha gritado que apenas quedan almas?
Acabo de encontrarme una con halo y todo,
dice que no soy mala y yo me tiro al suelo
y golpeo la tierra con mis puños abiertos.

De pronto se ha llenado mi monedero triste,
el pelo y la mirada se me ha puesto elegante.
Al diablo mis zapatos con las bocas abiertas,
hoy tengo nueva ave en mi corral piando.

I've Never Got Anything

I've never got anything in my gray purse,
never anything to dress up in,
always the same shoes without laces,
the same black shag to smoke, and I don't care.

There's a crystal nailed under my tongue
and a new being...Look, I'm going to talk about a new being.

What old idiot cried that there were no souls left?
I just met one with a halo and all,
who says I am O.K., so I throw myself down
and beat the earth with my open fists.

All of a sudden my sad purse filled,
my hair straightened and my looks shaped up.
To hell with these shoes with their tongues hanging out,
today a new bird sings in my cage.

Pienso Mesa y Digo Silla

Pienso mesa y digo silla,
compro pan y me lo dejo,
lo que aprendo se me olvida,
lo que pasa es que te quiero.
La trilla lo dice todo,
y el mendigo en el alero,
el pez vuela por la sala,
el toro sopla en el ruedo.
Entre Santander y Asturias
pasa un río, pasa un ciervo,
pasa un rebaño de santas,
pasa un peso.
Entre mi sangre y el llanto
hay un puente muy pequeño,
y por él no pasa nada,
lo que pasa es que te quiero.

I Think Table and I Say Chair

I think table and I say chair,
I buy bread and I lose it,
whatever I learn I forget,
and what this means is I love you.
The harrow says it all
and the huddled beggar,
the fish that flies through the living room,
the bull bellowing in his last corner.
Between Santander and Asturias
a river runs, deer pass,
a herd of saints passes,
a great load passes.
Between my blood and my tears
there is a tiny bridge,
and nothing crosses; what
this means is I love you.

De los Periódicos

Un guante de los largos,
siete metros de cuerda,
dos carretes de alambre
una corona de muerto
cuatro clavos,
cinco duros de plata
una válvula de motor
un collar de señora
unas gafas de caballero
un juguete de niño,
la campanilla de la parroquia
la vidriera del convento,
el péndulo de un reloj,
un álbum de fotografías
soldaditos de plomo
un San Antonio de escayola
dos dentaduras postizas
la ele de una máquina de escribir
y un guardapelo,
todo esto tenía el avestruz en su estómago.

From the Newspapers

A single glove, size large,
seven yards of string,
two spools of wire,
a funeral wreath,
four nails,
five silver coins,
an engine valve,
a woman's necklace,
a man's glasses,
a child's toy,
the parish church bell,
the window of the convent,
the pendulum of a clock,
a photograph album,
lead soldiers,
a plaster St. Anthony,
two sets of false teeth,
the "L" from a typewriter,
and a locket—
that's what the ostrich had in its stomach.

Ventanas Pintadas

Vivía en una casa
con dos ventanas de verdad y las otras dos pintadas en la fachada.
Aquellas ventanas pintadas fueron mi primer dolor.
Palpaba las paredes del pasillo,
intentando encontrar las ventanas por dentro.
Toda mi infancia la pasé con el deseo
de asomarme para ver lo que se veía
desde aquellas ventanas que no existieron.

Painted Windows

I lived in a house
with two real windows and the other two painted on.
Those painted windows caused my first sorrow.
I'd touch the sides of the hall
trying to reach the windows from inside.
I spent my whole childhood wanting
to lean out and see what could be seen
from the windows that weren't there.

El Alba Se Ha Puesto Fría

El alba se ha puesto fría
como la espalda de Elena,
que se murió por la tarde
de eso que la daba a ella.

El perro del hortelano
está ladrando en la acequia
donde ayer lloré y el llanto
se me convirtió en culebra.

No me duermo y ya la noche
da zancadas por la sierra,
mientras un toro muy débil
se aparece y me cornea.

The Dawn Has Turned as Cold

The dawn has turned as cold
as Helen's back,
who died toward afternoon
of the things that always got her.

The truck farmer's dog
is yapping down by the irrigation ditch
where yesterday I cried, and the crying
twisted into a snake.

I can't sleep, and now the night
is making tracks out on the sierra,
while a puny bull
comes on and gores me.

Chimenea de Leña

El fuego habla.
Algunos troncos chillan antes de morir,
otros como San Lorenzo se queman y en paz;
un coro de invisibles chicharras lanza su perorata
chirría la lumbre una canción desesperada,
—se me han enredado los ojos en las llamas—.
Carnaval,
los troncos están habitados,
la muchedumbre grita antes de disfrazarse de ceniza.

Fireplace

The fire speaks.
Some logs cry out before dying,
others like Saint Lawrence burn up in peace;
a chorus of invisible crickets delivers its oration,
the sparks hiss a desperate song,
— my eyes have gotten all tangled up in the flames.
Carnival time,
the logs are inhabited,
the crowds shriek before covering themselves in ashes.

Verbena

—Aquí está la gracia de las cosas sin gracia,
vean la mariposa que quiere ser estrella de cine,
lucha por ir a Hollywood y va a vivir un día;
sólo vale una mirada entrar a ver la gran tragedia.
Estas luces que veis sólo las veis vosotros,
dentro hay negros que nadan ríos espirituales.
—Es de noche y la foca canta a sus nietos nanas—.
— ¿Quieren ver una madre que parió una ternera?
— ¡Algo más importante que la mujer barbuda
os espera en la Tienda del Biombo!
—Este niño pequeño tiene cientos de siglos
y toca el violín con los brazos vendados,
que amar es preferible a vivir como tuerto.
—Es el triciclo loco, se sube por las tapias;
el gigante hace juegos de agua, es un niño;
y esta silla es eléctrica y puede dar corriente.
—Aquí está la Paquita que le adivina el sino.
¿Quién quiere saber todo lo que será mañana?
—la Paquita se ha muerto y sigue adivinando—
—hagan cola, señores, porque el dragón no tiene—.
¡Habitantes del mundo, pasad a la cabaña
que se exhibe un poeta, pasad al circo mudo,
tenemos caballitos de todos los colores,
tenemos tiro al blanco, tenemos mucha hambre!
—acérquense al quirófano y coman algodón—.
El aire tiene polvo de chulos y ladrones.
(Se ha roto el organillo, el chotis sale vals).
— ¡Este cerebro mágico recuerda lo que debe!
¡Entren, vean la monja que bebe más coñac!
—El faquir Manolito que mastica bombillas.
—El gusano de seda que obedece
y la cabra Paloma que rebuzna.
—Habitantes del barrio, pasad a la montaña,
os ha hablado un Profeta—ahora empieza a llover.

Verbena (Saint's Day Festival, Madrid)

—Here is the soul of things without soul,
see the butterfly that wants to be a movie star,
though it lives only one day it struggles to get to Hollywood;
to enter and see the great tragedy costs only a look.
You see these lights, only you see them,
inside are Negroes who swim in rivers of spirituals.
—It is night, and the seal sings lullabies to her grandsons.
—Do you want to see a woman who gave birth to a heifer?
—In the big tent you wait for something
more spectacular than the bearded woman!
—This little kid is hundreds of centuries old
and plays the violin with bandaged arms,
because to love is better than living as a one-eyed man.
—Here's the crazy tricycle that climbs the walls;
this giant plays with water and is a child;
this chair is electric and shocking.
—Here is La Paquita, who reads the future.
Who wants to know everything that's coming tomorrow?
—La Paquita is dead and goes on predicting the future—
Form the tail, people, that the dragon hasn't got.
All you people of the world, come to the tent,
here is a poet on exhibit, here is the silent circus,
we have little horses of every color,
we have target shooting, we are starving!
—step into the operating room and eat bandages like candy.
The air holds the dust of punks and thieves.
(The barrel organ is busted, the tango comes out a waltz.)
—This magic brain remembers what it must!
Come in and see the nun who gulps the most cognac!
—The fakir Manolito, who chews light bulbs.
—The silkworm trained to do tricks
and the Paloma goat who brays like an ass.
—All of you who live on this block, climb the mountain,
the Prophet has spoken to you—now it's beginning to rain.

Nací para Poeta o para Muerto

Nací para poeta o para muerto,
escogí lo difícil
—supervivo de todos los naufragios—
y sigo con mis versos,
vivita y coleando.

Nací para puta o payaso,
escogí lo difícil
—hacer reír a los clientes desahuciados—
y sigo con mis trucos,
sacando una paloma del refajo.

Nací para nada o soldado,
y escogí lo difícil
—no ser apenas nada en el tablado—
y sigo entre fusiles y pistolas
sin mancharme las manos.

I Was Born to Be a Poet or a Stiff

I was born to be a poet or a stiff,
I chose the hard way
— I survive all my shipwrecks —
and I go on writing,
alive and swinging.

I was born to be a whore or a clown,
I chose the hard way
— making the condemned customers laugh —
and I go on turning my tricks,
pulling pigeons from under my skirts.

I was born to be nothing or a soldier
and I chose the hard way
— to be less than nothing on the stage —
and I go on between rifles and revolvers
without bloodying my hands.

Oración para Ir Tirando

Padre nuestro que estás en los cielos
¿por qué no bajas y te das un garbeo?
Si te interesas por nuestros Fueros,
glorificado será tu abuelo.
Al obrerito y al palaciego
tus ordenanzas vienen al pelo.
—Hágase mi voluntad así en la mina
como en el lapicero. —

La "castaña" nuestra de cada día
dánosla hoy,
y disculpa nuestros ocios así como nosotros
"tragamos" a nuestros superiores
no nos dejes caer con el "tablón."

Mas líbranos del bien también.

Prayer to Keep Going

Our Father who art in heaven,
why don't you come down and take a look?
Hallowed be the name of your grandfather
if you'd take an interest in our rights.
Your ordinances fit like skin
on the little worker and the guy in his palace.
— Thy will be done in the lead
as in the pencil box! —

Give us this day
our daily whipping,
and forgive us our little flings
as we swallow those of our masters,
but don't let us puke on them.

Furthermore, deliver us from good.

Las Cosas

Las cosas, nuestras cosas,
las gusta que las quieran;
a mi mesa la gusta que yo apoye los codos,
a la silla la gusta que me siente en la silla,
a la puerta la gusta que la abra y la cierre
como al vino le gusta que le compre y le beba,
mi lápiz se deshace si le cojo y escribo,
mi armario se estremece si le abro y me asomo,
las sábanas, son sábanas cuando me echo sobre ellas
y la cama se queja cuando yo me levanto.

¿Qué será de las cosas cuando el hombre se acabe?
Como perros las cosas no existen sin el amo.

Things

These things, our things,
how they want to be wanted!
The table purrs under the weight of my elbows,
the chair is pleased when I sit in it,
the door asks to be opened and closed,
the wine to be purchased and drunk,
my pencil gives itself when I hold it and write,
the closet shudders when I open and peek,
the sheets are sheets when I stretch out,
the bed moans when I get up.

What will things be when we're finished?
They're like dogs that can't make it without their masters.

Ante un Muerto en Su Cama

¿Dónde estarán las abejas que hicieron la cera de tus cirios?
¿Dónde habrán ido a parar los primeros cuadernos que escribiste?
¿Dónde tu primera novia que no presiente que te has muerto?
¿En qué paisaje te has estremecido,
para ir a decirle que estás quieto?
(No es lo peor morirse, lo angustioso,
es que después, no puedes hacer nada,
ni dar cuerda al reloj,
ni despeinarte
ni ordenar los papeles...)

Te comprendo, estás triste.
—Intento consolarte.—
Si valiera decirte que te has muerto sobre tu cama limpia,
que tu alcoba la estaban rodeando los amigos
que se hizo todo lo posible por curarte
—que te estaban rayando la manzana—,
y que estaban bajándote el termómetro
y el más creyente rezaba muy bajito.
Piensa en los que no mueren en su casa,
en los que mueren de pronto en accidente,
o en esa mayoría que se van, en la guerra.
Ya han venido los de la Funeraria,
estás sobre una alfombra y tienes cuatro cirios,
un crucifijo blanco y un coro de vecinas;
que no te falta nada
y que estás muy bien peinado.

To a Dead Man in His Bed

Where are the bees that made the wax for these candles?
What became of the first diaries you wrote?
What became of the sweetheart who didn't foresee your death?
Down what passage have you quivered
to announce at last that you've come to rest?
(Dying isn't the worst. The agony
is that afterward you can't do a thing,
can't even wind your watch,
mess your own hair, arrange your papers . . .)

I know, you're sad.
—I want to help you—
It might help to know you died in your own clean bed,
that your friends were around you,
that everything was done to save you—
they were grating apples,
and doing everything to lower your temperature
and the faithful were quietly praying.
Think of those who don't die at home,
who go suddenly in an accident,
think of all those who die in war.
They've already come from the funeral home,
they've stretched you out on a little rug with four candles,
a plain crucifix and a chorus of neighbors;
there's nothing missing
and your hair is perfect.

El Camello

(Auto de los Reyes Magos)

El camello se pinchó
con un cardo del camino
y el mecánico Melchor
le dio vino.
Baltasar
fue a repostar,
más allá
del quinto pino...
e intranquilo el gran Melchor
consultaba su "Longinos."

— ¡No llegamos
no llegamos
y el Santo Parto ha venido!
— son las doce y tres minutos
y tres reyes se han perdido.

El camello cojeando
más medio muerto que vivo
va espeluchando su felpa
entre los troncos de olivos.

Acercándose a Gaspar
Melchor le dijo al oído:
— Vaya birria de camello
que en Oriente te han vendido.

A la entrada de Belén
al camello le dio hipo.
¡Ay qué tristeza tan grande
en su belfo y en su tipo!

Se iba cayendo la mirra
a lo largo del camino,

The Camel

(The Chevy of the Magi)

On the road the camel
was wounded by a thistle
and the mechanic Melchior
gave him some wine.
Balthazar
stopped to piss
way the hell
out there
and the great Melchior nervously
checked his Timex.

—We're not there yet,
we're not there
and the Child has arrived!
It's just past midnight
and the Three Kings are lost.

The camel, cringing,
more dead than alive,
runs crashing
against the olive trees.

Sidling up to Gaspar
Melchior whispered: What kind
of a lemon is this camel they
unloaded on you in the East?

At the gate of Bethlehem
the camel began to hiccup.
God, what grief rolled
from his lip to his rump!

Myrrh was leaking
all over the road,

Baltasar lleva los cofres,
Melchor empujaba al bicho.

Y a las tantas ya del alba
—ya cantaban pajarillos—
los tres reyes se quedaron
boquiabiertos e indecisos,
oyendo hablar como a un Hombre
a un Niño recién nacido.
—No quiero oro ni incienso
ni esos tesoros tan fríos,
quiero al camello, le quiero.
Le quiero—repitió el Niño.

A pie vuelven los tres reyes
cabizbajos y afligidos.

Mientras el camello echado
le hace cosquillas al Niño.

Balthazar lugged the coffers,
and Melchior pushed the wreck.

And long past dawn—
the little birds were already singing—
the Three Kings stood there
staring and uncertain,
hearing a Child just born
speak like a man.
—I don't want gold or incense
or these expensive meaningless gifts,
I want the camel, that's what I want,
I want the camel, the Child repeated

The Three Kings walked home
heads down and ashamed.

Meanwhile the fallen camel
began to tickle the Child.

El Día que se Implante la Paz

El día que se implante la paz, sobre la tierra
caerá una nevada tenaz y duradera,
todo será blanco de miradas en fiesta,
los copos serán grandes como sábanas cameras.
En aquella nevada Dios soltará sus banderas
y Cristo será feliz por vez primera.

The Day When Peace Takes Hold

The day when peace takes hold, a stubborn
and everlasting snow will fall upon the earth,
everything will be a target in our joyous sight,
the snowflakes will be as large as bed sheets.
In that snow God will unfurl his flags
and for the first time Christ will be happy.

Oración

Pasa,
no tengo más remedio que admitirte,
Tú eres el que viene cuando todos se van,
El que se queda cuando todos se marchan
El que cuando todo se apaga, se enciende.
El que nunca falta.
Mírame aquí,
sentada en una silla dibujando...
Todos se van, apenas se entretienen.
Haz que me acostumbre a las cosas de abajo,
dame la salvadora indiferencia,
haz un milagro más,
dame la risa,
¡hazme payaso, Dios, hazme payaso!

Prayer

Come in,
There's nothing else I can do but let you in;
You are the one who comes when everyone else goes,
the one who stays when everyone else leaves,
the one who ignites when the rest go out,
the one who never fails.
Look at me here,
sitting in a chair sketching...
Everyone's gone, they left without wasting time.
Help me get used to things as they are,
give me the indifference that will save me,
make one more miracle happen,
make me laugh,
make me a clown, dear God, make me a clown!

Oraciones Gramaticales

Yo tengo esperanza.
El perro tiene hambre.
El banco del jardín respira mal.
La niña se peina.
La vaca se lame.
Las cosas me miran,
es peor si me hablan.
En el suburbio hay flores maleantes.
Las macetas son botes,
los hombres son tigres,
los niños son viejos,
los gatos se comen,
las mondas también.
Los huérfanos huelen a madre.
Los pobres a humo.
Los ricos a brea.

Grammatical Sentences

I have hope.
The dog has hunger.
The garden bench breathes badly.
The young girl combs her hair.
The cow licks herself.
All things behold me
and it's worse if they talk to me.
The flowers in the suburbs are evil.
The flowerpots are boats,
the men are tigers,
the children have grown old,
the cats eat each other,
and pick the bones as well.
Orphans smell of their mothers,
the poor of smoke,
the rich of tar.

Estamos Bien

La mañana, se pierde en la maraña.
Por la tarde, los niños de la calle.
Por la noche, la radio del vecino.
La oficina me pone casi muerta.
El silencio se esconde en la repisa.
Yo no puedo leer una novela,
y la gata que pare en el pasillo
y mi hermano que no tiene trabajo
y la niña que llora por la esquina;
mi cuñada me pide una cebolla;
en la puerta, que llama el del recibo.
No hay quien pueda vivir cómodamente.
El tranvía no llega casi nunca
y no llega tampoco con el sueldo;
la merienda borróse de la casa;
el periódico nos dice la noticia:
se avecina, la garra de la guerra,
y yo digo: ¡Pues sí, lo que faltaba!

We're O.K.

Morning is lost in a maze.
By afternoon, kids in the street.
Night, the neighbor's radio.
The job is killing me.
Silence is somewhere else.
I can't read a book,
and the cat drops her kittens in the hall
and my brother with no work
and the little girl crying on the corner;
my sister-in-law wants an onion;
the bill collector bangs at the door.
No one can live like this.
The streetcar almost never arrives,
and my paycheck never arrives either;
lunch has vanished from the house;
now the papers bring us the news:
the paws of war claw nearer,
and I say: "Sure, just what we needed!"

Tu Parcela Tendrás

El caballo al morir tiene de todo,
¡el látigo se borra de su espalda!

No te acongojes, hombre,
que todo, nada dura.
Cuando llegue ese día,
el de mayor sosiego,
para entonces,
siempre habrá un árbol
que nos ofrezca amable cuatro tablas;
por pobre que seas, que hayas sido,
al final se te dará palmo de tierra
para que puedas tranquilo deshacerte.
Tu parcela tendrás
y podrás disponer de aquellas flores
que a otros muertos les lleve su familia.

You'll Get Yours

The dead horse has it all,
the whip is rinsed from his shoulders.

Don't be scared, man,
out of all this nothing lasts.
When that day
of supreme peace arrives
then
there will always be a tree
to offer us four friendly planks;
poor as you are or have been,
in the end you'll have your plot
where you can quietly fall apart.
You'll have your land
and you can command the flowers
brought to the others by their relatives.

Los Pájaros Anidan

Los pájaros anidan en mis brazos,
en mis hombros, detrás de mis rodillas,
entre los senos tengo codornices,
los pájaros se creen que soy un árbol.
Una fuente se creen que soy los cisnes,
bajan y beben todos cuando hablo.
Las ovejas me pisan cuando pasan
y comen en mis dedos los gorriones,
se creen que yo soy tierra las hormigas
y los hombres se creen que no soy nada.

Birds Nest

Birds nest in my arms,
on my shoulders, behind my knees,
between my breasts there are quail,
they must think I'm a tree.
The swans think I'm a fountain,
they all come down and drink when I talk.
When sheep pass, they pass over me,
and perched on my fingers, the sparrows eat,
the ants think I'm earth,
and men think I'm nothing.

Noticia

Porque a mí la Tristeza me perseguía
y me la encontraba hasta en la sopa,
he huido a la selva que no viene en el mapa,
y hasta aquí yo temo que me encuentre.
Lo temo porque recuerdo,
y no debiera recordar nada.
Porque hombre que quiere ser feliz,
debe hacerse un desvergonzado egoísta
y depilarse nombres de sus cejas,
y huir de la ciudad como yo hice.

No tengo más que un traje y un cuaderno
y mucho miedo a que se gaste el lápiz.

Al alba sólo al alba paso frío.

Me desvelan las aves y las hojas.

Vente conmigo cuando te harte todo.
Estoy en el alero de un frondoso
tocando el violón con una pluma.
Si te preguntan, no digas cualquier cosa.
Di que me perseguía la Tristeza
y busqué libertad en una isla
que no viene en el mapa.

News

Because sadness pursued me
and I kept meeting it even in my soup,
I've run away to the forest that's off the map,
and even here I'm afraid it will find me.
I'm afraid because I can't forget,
and I'd rather remember nothing.
Because if you want to be happy
you must become an egomaniac
and pluck names from your eyebrows
and run away from the city as I did.

I own nothing but a suit and a diary
and a great fear that my pencil will fail me.

At dawn, only at dawn, I get cold.

The birds and the leaves keep me awake.

Come join me when everything sickens you.
I'm under a roof of leaves
playing a violin with a feather.
If they question you, don't just say anything.
Say, Sadness pursued me
and I looked for freedom on an island
that's off the map.

About the Author

Gloria Fuertes is a Spanish poet and author of more than fifteen books of poetry. Born in 1918, she has been well known in Spain and Latin America for the past three decades. She has received several important prizes, including the Guipuzcoa prize for poetry and the Andersen prize for children's literature. Fuertes is the founder and director of *Arquero*, a Spanish poetry review. She lives in Madrid.

About the Translators

Born an identical twin in Detroit in 1928, Philip Levine held, from the age of fourteen, a variety of jobs, from assembling Cadillac transmissions to baking Wonder bread. He received a B.A. and an M.A. from Wayne State University, and an M.F.A. from the University of Iowa. His first book of poetry was published in 1963 and since then, he has written eight more, including *Not This Pig* (Wesleyan, 1968). *Ashes* (1979) and *Seven Years From Somewhere* (1979) won National Book Critics Circle awards, and *Ashes* also won the American Book Award in poetry in 1980. Levine is professor of English at Tufts University and at California State University at Fresno. His home is in Fresno.

Educated at Stanford University (B.A. 1967) and at SUNY/Albany (M.A. 1971; Ph.D. 1976), Ada Long received a grant in 1981 from the National Endowment for the Humanities to develop an interdisciplinary course sequence in the humanities. She has written extensively on women's literature and on many other aspects of world literature and poetry. She is the director of the university honors program at the University of Alabama at Birmingham, where she lives.

About the Book

Off the Map has been composed in Goudy Old Style by Carolinatype, printed on 70 lb. Warrens Olde Style by Edwards Brothers, and bound by Edwards Brothers.
Wesleyan University Press, 1984.